Dedicated with love to my cousin Dganit Barnea Sheffer,
her husband Liron and kids Bar, Reut & Gil.
I always love spending time with you all–
specifically at the chocolate store!

So said the great Rebbe of Kotzk
If I am I because you are you

and you are you because I am I

ואתה אתה כי אני אני

then I am not I

אז אני לא אני

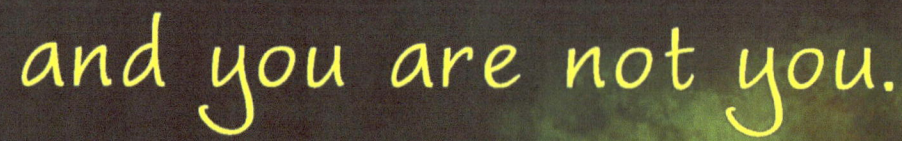

and you are not you.

וְאַתָּה לֹא אַתָּה.

אבל אם אני אני כי אני אני

and you are you
because you are you

ואתה אתה כי אתה אתה

then I am I and you are you.

אז אני אני
ואתה אתה

A yiddish proverb brilliantly articulated:

אם אהיה כמוה, מי תהיה כמוני

If I try to be like her, who will be like me?

פתגם יידישאי הטעים בתבונה:

Oscar Wilde gracefully
summed it up:

תהיו עצמכם
כל השאר כבר תפוסים

Be yourself; everyone else
is already taken.

אוסקר ווילד סיכם סיכם בחן:

The Great Rebbe of Kotzk

Menachem Mendel Morgensztern of Kotzk, better known as the Kotzker Rebbe (1787–1859) was a Hasidic Rabbi and leader.

Born to a non-Hasidic family in Goraj near Lublin, Poland, he became attracted to Hasidus in his youth.

He was known for having acquired impressive Talmudic and Kabbalistic knowledge at an early age. He was a student of Reb Bunim of Peshischa, and upon the latter's death attracted many of his followers.

The Kotzker Rebbe was well known for his incisive and down-to-earth philosophies, and sharp-witted sayings. Much like Captain Happiness, he appears to have had little patience for false piety or stupidity.

From 1839 he lived in seclusion for the last twenty years of his life.

Based on Wikepedia

Oscar Wilde (1854 – 1900) was an Anglo-Irish playwright, novelist, poet, and critic. He is regarded as one of the greatest playwrights of the Victorian Era. Besides literary accomplishments, he is also famous, for his wit, flamboyance, and affairs with men. He was tried and imprisoned for his homosexual relationship (then considered a crime) with the son of an aristocrat.

At the height of his fame and success, while his masterpiece, The Importance of Being Earnest (1895), was still on stage in London, Wilde had the Marquess of Queensberry prosecuted for libel. The Marquess was the father of Wilde's lover, Lord Alfred Douglas. The charge carried a penalty of up to two years in prison. The trial unearthed evidence that caused Wilde to drop his charges and led to his own arrest and trial for "gross indecency" with men. After two more trials he was convicted and imprisoned for two years' hard labour.

In 1897, in prison, he wrote De Profundis, which was published in 1905, a long letter which discusses his spiritual journey through his trials, forming a dark counterpoint to his earlier philosophy of pleasure. Upon his release he left immediately for France, never to return to Ireland or Britain. There he wrote his last work, The Ballad of Reading Gaol (1898), a long poem commemorating the harsh rhythms of prison life. He died in destitute in Paris at the age of 46.

Based on Wikipedia and http://www.wilde-online.info/oscar-wilde-biography.htm